If You Were Me and Lived in...
Ancient Greece

By Carole P. Roman

Illustrated by Mateya Arkova

For Alexander – you inspire me.

ISNB-10: 1-947118-17-X ISBN-13: 978-1-947118-17-1
Library of Congress Control Number: 2012921018
CreateSpace Independent Publishing Platform,
North Charleston, SC

This is an illustration of Greece today.

Greece may have looked like this in the year 350 B.C.

What are the differences?

Greece is located in the Mediterranean Sea in southeastern Europe at the crossroads between Asia, Africa, and Europe. It is officially known as the Hellenic Republic today and was called *Hellas* (Hel-las) in ancient times. The area has a long history dating back thousands of years. Greece was the first advanced civilization in the region, giving it the title of "the Cradle of Western Civilization." Ancient Greece created the foundation for many modern western societies, from legal and government systems to cultural features like literature and philosophy, as well as the Olympics.

Athens is currently the capital of Greece, and the first people settled there around the 11th-7th century B.C. That makes it one of the world's oldest cities.

9

If you were me and lived in Ancient Greece, you would be born around 2,300 years ago.

You would live sometime in the year 350 B.C. and during a time that would be called the Classical Period by historians. Your name could be *Alexandros* (Al-lex-an-dros) or *Linus* (Ly-en-us) if you were a boy. They might name your little sister *Melitta* (Me-lee-ta) or *Theodora* (Thee-uh-dor-ra).

You would be proud that Greece introduced a system of politics called *demokratia* (dem-ock-crat-ee-ya) or *ruled by the people*. The government had three institutions: a ruling body that wrote laws and handled foreign policy, a council of representatives from different tribes, and a court that argued cases. It became the model for democracy for the next two thousand years and Greece's most enduring contribution to the modern world.

If you were Greek, you would worship many gods. You would be taught that there were gods for every aspect of life. All the gods supposedly lived on a gigantic mountain called Mount Olympus. Its peak reaches 9,750 feet!

Zeus (Zoo-se) was the king of all the gods and was the strongest and wisest. He ruled over the Earth. *Hera* (Heh-ra), goddess of women and marriage, was his wife.

You might live in one of the several city-states that dotted the countryside. Some of the famous ones were Athens, Sparta, Argos, and Corinth. The people of these towns had a lot in common. They spoke the same language, which was Greek. They followed the same religion, yet if you asked someone where they came from, they never said Greece; they said the name of their city. A merchant from Athens would say he was Athenian; a farmer from Sparta would say he was Spartan. Even though they all knew they were Greek, they identified more with the towns where they lived.

Corinth

Athens

Argus

Sparta

Often, they banded together to fight foreign invaders, and sometimes they fought with each other when they had a dispute. All those battles created prisoners of war. Those prisoners became slaves and property of the people who captured them. Slavery was considered natural and part of everyday life. Slaves were important to the economy of Ancient Greece. Slaves worked on farms, in the mines, and in a trade as well as in households. Most homes had one to three slaves. At one point, it was thought there were more slaves than citizens in Athens. A slave could buy his freedom by paying what he was worth. He could never be enslaved once he was freed.

The Greek god of war was named *Ares* (Air-rees). He was a fierce fighter and the son of *Zeus* and *Hera*.

In Ancient Greece, you would probably live in a house made of stone or clay bricks that kept cool in the summer and warm in the colder weather. The floor would be hard-packed dirt. The house would have a central area with bedrooms, a kitchen, a room for bathing, and a separate dining room for your father to entertain his friends. Instead of a fireplace built into the wall, you would have a fire pit or hearth in the middle of the main room. Its coals burned all the time for both warmth and cooking. To honor the goddess *Hestia* (Hes-tee-ya), the coals were not allowed to be extinguished.

Your home usually had an open-air courtyard where you enjoyed the shade of the many olive trees. This was an important place in the Greek household, and your family gathered there to cook, sew, talk, and share meals. Do you have a room like that in your house today?

There weren't any words in the language of the Ancient Greeks that had the same meaning as the word "family." The closest word to family is the word "oikos" (oye-kos) which means household.

Every Ancient Greek city had a open fireplace for all citizens. *Hestia* was sacred there also. When the people of one city founded another city, they took coals with them to light the new city's hearth. Similar to fireplaces in private homes, the fires in public hearths were never allowed to die out.

Hestia (Hes-tee-ya) was the goddess of the home. Her name means hearth or fireplace. Every house had a fireplace to cook the food or keep the home warm.

Most days, your diet would consist of bread, cheese, olives, figs, and grapes. There was usually a lot of fish available, but meat was only eaten on special feast days when you were celebrating something special. Four meals were served a day: breakfast, mid-day meal, early evening snack, and finally dinner. For breakfast, everybody ate the same thing, which was bread dipped in wine. Sometimes they added figs and olives. They ate barley and lentils with the evening meal.

You did not like to drink plain water. Your mother told you it brought disease, so she mixed it with wine to kill off germs. Grapes were used to make the beverage, and there would be watered-down wine at every meal.

If your parents were wealthy and served formal dinners, your father ate separately from your mother. He reclined on a cushion and had to use only one hand to feed himself.

Your family never used napkins. Instead, they wiped their hands on bread that was later given to the dogs as meals.

There was no sugar in Ancient Greece. Instead, you kept and took care of a beehive in the back of the house. This way you would always have honey for dessert.

Demeter (Da-me-ter) was the goddess of corn, grain, and the harvest. It was believed she made the crops grow, and you would always offer the first loaf of bread made from the harvest to her. She was also called *Mother Earth* or *Mother Nature*.

Your father, especially was head of the house and made all the rules. Your mother did not have much to say and had to listen to him, just like you. If he was not rich, he might be a worker in a shop in the city. He would be called a *thetes* (the-tes) and would not be considered important in town. He might work at a forge and make weapons. He could be a craftsman who molded pottery from clay. He would create beautiful jugs and plates that were exported all over the world.

He could be a fisherman or a farmer who sold what he caught or grew to the people who lived in the city. He might also be a soldier or a city official.

If he owned a lot of land, he probably managed a large home called an estate and that meant you were wealthy.

If you found your home in Sparta, your father lived in barracks with other soldiers and only came home to visit your mom. If you were a boy, you went to live in a dormitory with other boys as soon as you turned seven years old. You stayed in the army until you were the age of sixty! Your sister stayed in a dormitory with girls, learning how to wrestle and fight too. Your sole job was to be brave, strong, and a good soldier. You didn't even have to work on the family farm. The people who were captured in battle did that.

Athena (A-thee-na) was the goddess of courage and wisdom. She never got mad quickly or without a reason. She believed in law and order, and you would hope her calm temperament influenced your father. Especially when you told him you wrecked the chariot.

If you were a boy in Ancient Greece in most of the city-states, you would be educated at home until you turned six years old. Next you would start school where they would teach you how to read and write. You would take classes in science and math and enjoy learning how to debate. The intention was to make you into a well-rounded and responsible citizen. Your favorite class would be music, where you learned how to play an instrument like a *lyre* (ly-er) or flute.

If you were a girl, you were not considered a citizen so would stay at home with your mother and grandmother to learn about running a household. You would be taught sewing, cooking, and purchasing things your home would need. If you were lucky, your mother might teach you to read and write.

Apollo (A-pol-lo) was the god of music. He was the twin brother of *Artemis* (Ar-tim-es), the goddess of the hunt. He was often pictured playing a golden lyre.

Most people in Ancient Greece wore the same type of clothes. You would probably wear a *chiton* (khit-ōn) which was a long, bleached white shirt-like garment that your mother sewed. The *peplos* (pep-luhs) was the draped garment that women wore. Men wrapped them selves in a toga (to-ga). The clothes were rather plain, wool in the winter and airy linen for the summer. Sometimes they used dyes from plants to make the garments brightly colored. Mothers would create geometric designs to identify the town of their origination.

You and your family would love jewelry and wore bracelets, rings, and pins filled with precious stones from countries far away. Traders brought products from Asia and the Middle East to the ports of Greece. Both of your parents wore perfume made from local plants.

In some city-states, men wore their hair long and luxurious, putting on ointments and saying their hair was an ornament. In other cities, boys cut their hair when they turned thirteen. Either way, you would brush your hair often and for a long time. Whether you were a boy or a girl, your hair would be complimented for its thick and healthy shine. Its condition was important. Your mother and sisters wore golden or silk hairnets and other kinds of beautiful jewelry in their hair.

Your father and uncles had bushy beards and were proud of them. Beard trimming became an art and barbers were important. For the ancient Athenians, the beard was a sign of manhood and strength.

Aphrodite (Af-ro-digh-tee) was the goddess of love and beauty. She loved the myrtle tree, and her favorite birds were the dove and swan.

You would buy your clothes and other products in the *agora* (a-gor-a) or marketplace. Agora means "gathering place" and would be an area in your town where athletic, religious, and political activities would take place. Merchants set up stalls to sell their products. It was an ideal area to hear what was going on or buy the latest products. Shepherds sold cheeses; farmers brought their crops of barley and olives to trade. Women sold ribbons and perfume. Spices from India were found next to ivory from Africa; there was also linen from Egypt to make light clothing for the hot summers. There were no set prices, so when you went shopping, you came prepared to haggle. Can you guess what that means?

Hermes (Her-mes) was the god of herdsmen, trade, roads, and travelers. He had wings on his helmet and feet.

34

Greece was a civilized society that used its fleet of ships to bring valuable products and ideas from all over the world. They traded with China, the Middle East, and Africa. You used coins made from a mix of gold and silver that were mined in the hills of Greece. They were called *drachmas* (drach-mas). Using money in exchange for products was an important invention. It provided a way to hire soldiers and pay people for goods or services. It made it easy to travel long distance with something valuable to trade. Imagine traveling with heavy cheeses or squawking chickens if you wanted to trade for cloth from a merchant in another city. Which would you rather carry - a dozen chickens or a dozen coins?

Poseidon (Po-sigh-don) was the god that ruled the seas. He supposedly calmed the waters or made fierce storms. He drove a golden cart called a chariot. It was pulled by mythological creatures that were half-horse, half-snakes. Poseidon carried a three-pointed spear called a trident. He used it to start earthquakes or bring water out of the ground.

The Olympics were created in Greece thousands of years ago and held every four years. All the city-states sent their athletes to compete and make their town look the best. If you were me and lived in Ancient Greece, you would practice every day so that you would win the chariot race or the wrestling match because you would want a poem to be written about your incredible strength.

Heracles (He-ra-cleese) was the hero of great strength. He was *Zeus's* son and half-god and half-human. He was the greatest of the Greek heroes, an example of power as well as a champion. In Rome and the modern West, he was known as *Hercules* (Her-cu-lees).

If you were me and born in Ancient Greece, you would be proud to point out that democracy was founded there. The Greeks were the first elected officials to make the laws around 500 BC.

You may boast that three of the greatest philosophers came from Greece, and their lessons are still taught today. *Plato* (Plae-to) started the first school of higher learning in the western world. *Socrates* (Soc-ra-teez) set the foundation for studying philosophy and science, and *Aristotle* (Ar-ris-tot-el) promoted views on physics that shaped the way people have learned for the last two thousand years.

You would love reminding people that *Hippocrates* (Hip-pock-ra-tees) is the father of modern medicine. He wrote a vital set of rules for doctors to follow over two thousand years ago. It is one of the oldest documents in the world.

You would love to pull out your copies of *The Iliad* (Ill-ye-ad) and *The Odyssey* (Od-des-see) and discuss their author, *Homer* (Ho-mer). He was one of the first recorded poets in the world.

You might have read about the exploits of Alexander the Great, the young king of *Macedon* (Ma-cee-don) which was part of Greece, and how he conquered his enemies. He never lost a single battle, even when outnumbered. Even today military schools use his tactics to teach new soldiers. Over twenty cities in the world were named after him.

GODS & GODDESSES OF ANCIENT GREECE

Aphrodite (Af-ro-digh-tee)- goddess of love who was responsible for starting the Trojan (Tro-jun) War. She caused Queen Helen of Troy to fall in love with the rival prince of Sparta which began the conflict.

Apollo (A-pol-lo)- god of wisdom, music, and poetry. He was the twin of Artemis.

Ares (Air-rees)- god of war. He was a bully and cruel. Ares liked suffering and was a rather unpleasant fellow.

Artemis (Ar-tim-es)- goddess of the hunt and the phases of the moon. She protected small animals.

Athena (A-thee-na)- goddess of wisdom. The city of Athens was named after her. She was a wise warrior, and her symbol was an owl.

Demeter (Da-me-ter)- goddess of the harvest, grains, and fertility. She is often referred to as Mother Earth. When her daughter, Persephone (Per-sef-e-ne), was taken to Hades, Demeter searched for her and neglected the harvest. The fields died out. Zeus made a deal with Hades that Persephone would spend six months with her mother above ground and six months below with him, creating the seasons.

Hades (Hay-des)- god of the underworld and in charge of keeping the dead there. He drove a chariot with four dark horses.

Hestia (Hes-tee-ya)- goddess of the hearth or home. She held the keys to Mount Olympus.

Hephaestus (He-fay-tus)- god of fire. He made the famous Pandora's box from clay. She opened a forbidden container, letting out the evils in the world, and as a result, when a person *"opens a Pandora's box,"* it means he or she causes a lot of trouble.

Hera (Heh-ra)- queen of the gods and protector of women. Hera was married to Zeus. She was bossy, and once when someone disagreed with her, she turned them into a crane, which is a bird that lives near water.

Hermes (Her-mes)- god of herdsmen, trade, roads, merchants, messengers, and travelers. It was said he invented the first musical instrument when he placed a string across a turtle shell. They say he created music that day too!

Poseidon (Po-sigh-don)- god of the sea. He would be calm and reasonable or angry and cause storms and earthquakes. He was famous for destroying the mythical city of Atlantis because the people there did not respect him. He was important in Greece because there were a lot of fishermen living there.

Zeus (Zoo-se)- king of all gods who ruled the Earth. He was a father to many of the younger gods and sometimes could be mean and thoughtless. He gave justice and laws to the mortals. He encouraged them to be kind to each other. He controlled the weather and could make thunder and lightning strike, making him the most powerful of all the gods.

So you see, if you were me,
how life in Ancient Greece could really be.

Glossary

agora (a-gor-a)- a gathering place or marketplace.

Alexandros (Al-lex-an-dros)- a popular boy's name in Ancient Greece.

Argos (Ar-gos)- a city-state in Ancient Greece.

Aristotle (Ar-ris-tot-el)- a great teacher and philosopher.

Athens (Ath-ens)- a city-state in Ancient Greece.

Athenians (Ath-en-ee-ans)- the people who lived in Athens.

Atlantis (At-lan-tis)- the fabled city that sank into the sea.

barley (bar-lee)- a cereal grain, part of the grass family. Barley is commonly used in soups, stews, and distilled drinks.

barracks (ba-racks)- a place where soldiers live and sleep together.

B.C.- stands for Before Christ, and it means the number of years before the time of Jesus Christ. That was about 2000 years ago, so the date 350 B.C. means 2366 years ago. Some people use B.C.E. instead. That stands for Before the Common Era and is used in order to avoid religious references.

chariot (cha-ree-et)- a cart pulled by horse for transport.

chiton (khit-ōn)- a long, bleached white shirt-like garment worn by both men and women in Ancient Greece.

citizen (cit-a-zen)- a person living in a city-state that has responsibilities and rights.

city-states (cit-tee-states)- small towns that governed the territory surrounding their city.

civilization (civ-il-i-za-tion)- a group of people that develops into an advanced and organized society.

Corinth (Cor-neeth)- a city-state in Greece.

craftsman (crafts-man)- a person who creates useful or beautiful objects.

crane (crane)- a long-legged bird that lives near water.

democracy (dem-ock-ra-cee)- the government ruled by elected officials by the citizens.

demokratia (dem-ock-crat-ee-ya)- means "people of the power." Demokratia is a direct democracy of people who want a say in their government policies.

dormitory (dor-mi-tor-ree)- the place where boys were housed to train to be soldiers.

drachmas (drach-mas)- the currency used in ancient Greece before the euro was introduced.

estate (es-state)- a large home of a wealthy citizen.

flute (flut)- a side-blown wind instrument, usually made of metal.

forge (forj)- a fireplace used to make metal objects by heating the metal, making it easy to shape using a hammer.

geometric (gee-o-me-trik)- using shapes or lines to make a design.

hairnets (hair-nets)- woven nets worn to contain hair, often used as decoration.

hearth (harth)- the flooring of a fireplace.

Hellenic Republic- (He-len-ik Re-pub-lic)- the official name for Greece.

Hellas (Hel-las)- the name by which Greece was known in ancient times.

Hippocrates (Hip-pock-ra-tees)- the father of modern medicine.

Homer (Ho-mer)- the first known poet to write epic poems. He wrote *The Iliad* and *The Odyssey*.

jug (juhg)- a clay vessel used to hold liquids.

lentils (len-tils)- a plant from the legume or bean family used as food.

Linus (Ly-en-us)- a popular boy's name in Ancient Greece.

lyre (ly-er)- a stringed instrument like a harp.

Macedon (Ma-cee-don)- also known as Macedonia, it is an ancient kingdom that was part of Greece.

Melitta (Me-lee-ta)- a popular girl's name in Ancient Greece.

Mount Olympus (Uh-lim-pus)- a giant mountain where people believed the gods lived.

myrtle (mur-tul)- a beautiful flowering tree with bright purple flowers.

oikos (oye-kos)- loosely interpreted as the Greek word for family.

Olympics (Uh-lim-pics)- organized games where city-states send their best athletes to compete against each other every four years.

Pandora's box (Pan-dor-uh's box)- a mythical story about a girl who opens a forbidden box, unleashing evil on the world.

peplos (pep-luhs)- a draped garment worn by women.

philosophers (fi-las-so-fers)- the people who study culture and why people do the things they do.

philosophy (fil-las-so-fee)- the study of life, culture, and the reasons people do what they do.

physics (fiz-iks)- the study of motion using time, space, and energy.

Plato (Plae-to)- a great Greek teacher and philosopher who founded the first academy of higher education.

Socrates (Soc-ra-teez)- one of the greatest teachers of all time. He introduced many ideas in philosophy and rational thought to the Western world.

Sparta (Spar-ta)- a city-state in Ancient Greece.

Spartan (Spar-tan)- the people who lived in Sparta.

Theodora (Thee-uh-dor-ra)- a popular girl's name in ancient Greece.

The Iliad (The Ill-yee-ad)- the story of the Trojan War written by Homer.

The Odyssey (Od-uh-see)- the continuation of *The Iliad*, the return trip of the great warrior Odysseus from the Trojan War.

thetes (the-tes)- common workers who were paid in food and clothing.

trident (tri-dent)- a three-pronged spear.

Trojan War (Tro-jun War)- the epic twelve-year battle when Queen Helen of Sparta ran away to be with the Prince of Troy, Paris.

togas (to-ga)- a draped garment worn by citizens.

wisdom (wiz-dom)- the quality of having enough knowledge and experience to make correct decisions.

underworld (un-der-world)- place where the dead stay.

Please visit my blog for additional resources for this book and others, including printable worksheets, coloring pages topics for essays, and critical thinking.

caroleproman.blogspot.com

CPSIA information can be obtained
at www.ICGtesting.com
Printed in the USA
BVHW020307190721
612088BV00002B/9